Zeal

Andrew Bailey

Zeal

ENITHARMON PRESS

First published in 2012
by Enitharmon Press
26B Caversham Road
London NW5 2DU

www.enitharmon.co.uk

Distributed in the UK by
Central Books
99 Wallis Road
London E9 5LN

Distributed in the USA and Canada
by Dufour Editions Inc.
PO Box 7, Chester Springs
PA 19425, USA

ISBN: 978-1-907587-20-7

Enitharmon Press gratefully acknowledges the
financial support of Arts Council England.

British Library Cataloguing-in-Publication Data.
A catalogue record for this book is available
from the British Library.

Volume 5 in the Enitharmon New Poets series,
dedicated to the memory of Alan Clodd (1918–2002)
and generously funded by his estate.

Designed in Albertina by Libanus Press
and printed in England by
Antony Rowe Ltd

ACKNOWLEDGEMENTS

Some of these poems have previously been published in *Brittle Star, Cake, Exultations and Difficulties, Eyewear, Facebook Poetry, The Long Poem Magazine, nthposition, Poetry Review, Route 57, Stand, Stride, The Rialto,* and *Vallum* (Canada). 'Going to the Chapel' appears in *Lifemarks* (2007), an anthology in support of the Motor Neurone Disease Association, 'Honeymoon Sketchbook' appears in *Kaleidoscope* (2011), and 'Pica' in *Said and Done* (2011).

Many friends and family members deserve gratitude for their support and criticism, particularly George Ttoouli, Jo Bell, Derek Adams and Arthur Gardner, whose eyes for my blind spots have caught many faults. Thanks are also due to Elaine Feinstein and Penelope Shuttle.

CONTENTS

QUICKENING

Where surf fusses at the definitions
      of sandy water, watery sand, a tethered boat
            enjoys support from both.
I promised once to sail,
      one hand in sea one hand in sky,
            for the point where they would meet
and I would learn some undefined
      but Eleusinian thing. I learned
            about how to be wet. The boat
dozes at its leash, grasses bind
      the dune grains, and driftwood relaxes
            to its dry weight. That fuss at my ankles,
accidental signage of the water's
      lunar schedule. I have an inland train
            to catch tonight and do not
want to, do not want to take my feet
      from the quickened sands accepting them
            as the sea's further edge will soon the sun.

DREAM

Dream is headfill, is only infrequent or forgotten.
What there is is rarely image, but instant knowledge
mainlined to backbrain – you have seen this, said this,
only now, dream is a shark while pinned to the raft,
the rafters of its gullet gothic and closing.

The place to which the world goes as eyes close
is where the laws come from, is why there are none;
that you cannot move is common, common as birth
and an offer of that, don't wake, accept the stillness,
the invite written in your immobility, and belong.

Dream is a thread from the invisible who want you,
it can lead you, but if you fight will break.
Do not wake. Do not try to. Let the teeth close,
you will see the vaulted arches spin around your sight,
a kaleidoscope of vision solely yours. Sleep.

LODESTAR, POLESTAR

i.m. Peter Redgrove

Although he is now become lodestar, the water
that flooded the village I lived in was him
and still is him, for steeped in his substance
as I climbed the moonlit path from the water-village,
where the moonlight that lit the way was him,
my moondried self stayed redolent of him.

The north star sings: for you he is with me now.

Then I discipled myself to these uncommandments,
tried to find the stars in sunlit skylights, the doors
to dreams that do not leave or let you close them,
to other minds that fan and close like tarot decks;
I still endeavour, master, to be beesize, mothsize,
or so massive that the flesh that carries you can
seethe the dreams of mice from its pores to join
the tiny bestiaries choiring metamorphoses
among the grasses. The north star sings for me.

The stars that fall fall just as rain, and their ashes
dust clouds, making rain of him; the rain
makes plants of him, and so until we share him,
share his light, which holds still to that star
about which other stars, that are, as we are, him, rotate.

HYDROTHERAPY

as
gods play
on sanctus strings

healing
fingers bring
liquid upon you

spilt
down after
down cliff after

cliff
without plan
to basin a

place
to rest
to rust from

one
hour to
next in salts

silt
scatter of
light and elect

pain
is not
granted to us

prayer
thrives in
lit air O

holy
spirits you
walk up there

CALCULATE

And if I will raise hands empty of stars,
      forgive me.

And if I am through being fed by the rain,
wound round limited material need,
      forgive me.

And should I come to the river where questions
are washed away under waternymph murmurs,
of fearful mechanical measures of wealth,
      forgive me.

In wind and windfalls; in the imperatives of words;
in front of distant thunderheads, of empty stars
considering their way from me; those moments
you wanted wrapped round the flesh are flesh,
      forgive me.

Silence by little silence fills my windfall nest
fortified with shadow for the mud. I am
out of starlight, empty of rain, a calculation
rattled on the riverbed, where the wrong jewels
flash their must-have figures. My sleeping stars,
      forgive me.

TRANSPARENT

As the transparency of water bends whatever
it accepts, as that of ghosts chills, love,
as mine, is transparent, as is gravity. And you,
the shine of you shining, sky-scented,
do not see through me, but lift me weightless,
bring me solidity, you bring translucence out.

MORNING SONG

for eyes to open so
her thigh across my thigh
arm to one shoulder
head on the other
I the flotsam
to her Gulliver
exactly as they shut:
shipwrecked
in our stillness

AT THE KETTLE

galactic movement
milk beneath tea surface
ghost dances

HALLOWEEN

a cobweb past noon
        we barely saw
                in the hymn and butchery

of Grand Central Station
        him opening a braid to her
                marry me?

her little klaxons yes
        yes yes yes
                hands noding spidersilk

too private? too joyful
        brisk lunch pumpkin masks
                lanterneyed by yes

a yes no secret at all

the big intended *and* impending and no fear
though films insist, no vault instead
with exultation over sofa, oh my stated other
oh my same, with heart as willing here's
all intimate in intended memories my hand

lovely and loving and loved and in reverence
before one another, at least I before you, you
have with your *yes* kicked off a teleology
so, though so much done, so however much,
is still no dent in the set of all things to do

and *all* done without you counts now
undone, can never do everything, no, but can leap
in intent on everything shrinking and small
as is possible, smaller and smaller and
small as we can and what's next?

HONEYMOON SKETCHBOOK

failing to fall
asleep my wife's
right thigh in
  my new
  left hand

~

you look for the chin while shaving
or later checking – no surprise –
but when you lean to neaten up
a tie's dimple this clean face leaps out;
so this thin ring, so – cutesy,
but what better excuse – so love

~

confetti forbidden, but later
inordinate butterflies

~

ba-fucking-lloons!
 and laughter
 something spectacular

~

diagonal in driveway
fallen champagne cork

~

a bat last night
emptying the space
  by the house
of its insects swoops
so close it startles

not so close
as to drive her away
from the seeing of it

~

there is a transfinite
number of things I enjoy
less than eating sushi
on a train with you

~

wind farm at fleetwood
far enough to seem
nigh on imaginary
pale against pale
and still beautiful
as is wife

~

there has not yet been a day without rain;
this past half-hour has been a space without sky,
and rainfall reaches us heavy, white noise
over flagstones deepening a glaze to instants
of darning mushrooms, upsplashes for handles,

but behind the no sky there was cloud,
white cloud, that comes to be usual
as the nothing detaches, passes over,
gives way to horizon, to texture,
to even the blue between

~

−shall I fetch a glass of water?
−you just need to lie there,
she said, beam out love,
that's all I need

~

and now
I can run to seed
I mean to fat

COUPLETS IN BLUE

I kissed, I suppose, the baked apples
beneath your bathrobe – and

the rising water blued the shreds
of the bay, flooded the fish.

        Aspects of
        no matter
        the time.

Children's fireworks on replay
so slow on blueness.

Ignore what will surely betray me;
things are now, they will ever.

SOMEONE ELSE'S BABY

yawns its distraction wet
red diamond alive as an ovary
no small change, no chance,
sunshine a drum beneath
the grass above my ears
clatters out of ghosts

ungiven kisses fall
whatever the asphodels

the lizard and undeserved
thing of me poor creature
half-finished licking the vacuum
yawns its own goddess
the blood, a cord, slips
a fist a pulse beneath
infinite maybe fruit
raining down together

ungiven kisses fall
whatever the asphodels

infant infested field
small moons orbiting
asphodels as soft as
this hand of mist miles
from our daffodils
vased for valentine

ungiven kisses fall
whatever the asphodels

HERB ROBERT

'. . . no-one can legally claim that *the herb is a cancer cure*. No scientific
research has been done that shows it can cure any ailment.' *Middle Path
Awareness Sanctuary website*

The great Dioscorides has already described it.
An irrepressible, joyous addition to any garden.
Will add beauty, health, healing wherever it goes.
Thousandweed. Staunchweed. Nosebleed.

It has this wide range of applications in the home
and clinic: astringent, antibiotic, antiviral,
styptic, tonic, diuretic, Foetid Cranesbill. Stinky Bob.
Note it only smells like foxes, the flavour

is not unpleasant. Old-Man's-Pepper. Digestive,
sedative, antioxidant. Dog's Toe. The dog
made a full recovery. Felonwort.
Soothing to bladder pains, neuralgia,

Fox Geranium. Yarroway. Cuckoo's Eye.
bruises, fistulas, and skin problems.
Crobh Dearg. The lumps are going.
The new x-rays showed not one sign.

Soldier's Woundwort. No insect pest bothers it.
Granny-Thread-the-Needle. Stinking Jenny. Her life
was now free of any sign of it, which Mary believes
was due, entirely, to taking herb robert daily.

Hop o'-My-Thumb. Puck. Robin-i'-the-Hedge
The nodes started to recede and diminish in size,
Wren's Eye. Devil's Nettle. Dragonsblood.
till they were completely gone. Bloodwort.

Redshanks. Death-come-quickly. Don't. Saint Robert. Neighbouring plants are healthier and more vigorous.

OGRES

And there there is a lemon that contains
    an island where they laugh so loud it hurts –
the souls of all the ogres in Ceylon

have been secreted far enough from harm
    that they assume their soulless frames immortal.
But there there is a lemon that contains

the path to the secret citrus grove, wherein
    assurances were made that seemed to state
the souls of all the ogres in Ceylon

would be protected. And there, too, to be found
    is a blunted knife, an x-marked chart,
and there there is a lemon that contains

a lemon-scented sharpening stone
    that hones the sour knife till it could halt
the souls of all the ogres in Ceylon.

And there's that grove, that path, that laugh again.
    You grip the knife, your other hand out flat,
and there there is a lemon that contains
the souls of all the ogres in Ceylon.

TOUCH

Of being taken care of: we look for touch
and fear unhygiene, cracking knuckles
wringing hands, all tactile but virtual
    when haptic solo.

We crave touch, not that we should,
now hands are licensed, reputable masseurs.
No-one is more aware of the importance
    of touch than you.

There was always work. The work always
centred on fear of the dark, and sex is not
necessarily touch: *viz.* waking to memory
    of total mistake,

we couldn't open up for one another,
partner gone or died or grown sick, therefore
touch is not natural, often aggressive,
    putting one hand on my arm.

These people, they're in negative,
with not-hands, the touch untouched:
they're lost like they're in dreamland,
    yearning for touch.

This encouraged to exist a negative
touch, touch that says intense
to many serotonin-touched, heads touching
    under covers

to say please hands that allow
amazed sex stopped against need
and whole-body contact as if
    no years old.

SUCCUBUS

Woke to a gathering thightaut clamp of orgasm
gearing up and gritted teeth to gather back
the scrambling life to its slackening vesicles,

disobedient to the call of an unseen dream
of seraglio whence she, not flesh, just light,
left her touch, rays through rose windows,
still warm across me approaching back asleep,

where a vision, an infant, laughs, reaches up
to draw me down or him up and kisses me,
half light half you he says and bears a new dream in –

the airborne infant leads me floating through
the shelves of a library with no doors out
to a book that falling open starts
the airborne infant leads me floating through
the shelves of a library with no doors out.

PHARSALIAN SENTENCES

Around Sabellus' near-invisible wound the flesh dissolved to blood,
to bare the pale bone and failing organs, from the poison of the seps.

Aulus desiccated by the parching painless bite of a dipsa.
The Marsian farmer rose like dough, burst his armour, from
      the Prester's bite.

Murrus felt the fatal basilisk's venom reach his lethal lance-hand,
unsheathed his sword left-handed, and severed his lost arm at
      the shoulder.

AND SAND

And sand insinuates itself
    without exhaustion, as the dust
is drawn to dust; it starts in stealth
    and ends in dunes drawn over us

SANDCASTING

Allowing the sand to fall sand through my fingers
the distance dissolves like the sand through my fingers
sandalwood cardamom sand through my fingers

I feel your breath breathe the sand through my fingers
I make out your body in sand through my fingers
patchouli neroli sand through my fingers

I breathe you surround me sand through my fingers
ylang-ylang frankincense sand through my fingers

I powder I drift I am sand through my fingers
we touch all we are we are sand of our fingers
ylang-ylang sandalwood cinnamon sand

COASTAL

Scatter your talk in the clutter
of cuttlebones and crabshells,
go discalced over kelp and laver,

pick the secret language up
of the silicate scratch and tickle
through your delicate soles,

of clutch, lick and suck back
of bladderwrack slumped thick
over rockpools also. Salt will cleanse
and thicken the flesh of your feet,

will coarsen the skin to cuneiform,
each scale articulate,
grit over interlocutors.

We will speak like sandpaper,
sharkskin flesh scoring phrases
in abrasive clinching, scraping,

tongues licked into silence
by this close, serrated eloquence.

ASPIRE

each particle of sand aspires
to pearl;
    such sparse, selective oysters

SERÂB

Softening on the tongue, the cactus spine
grows succulent, its poisons sublimate
to psilocybin across the button
that dissolves to mezcal in your gut.
In the sands the truth feels safe enough
to show itself and sand-dunes staircase
to Babylon shelves, the ground exhales green,
flowers seethe from sparkling creepers, secrets
unsheathe from hollows in the palms of leaves.

A lake seeps mercury from a million pores;
from lapping ripples zebras coalesce.

Hold up your palm, let it grow
unfamiliar, a leathered square flexing
hidden veins to its own beat. Drop it
in the lake, drown its twitching bulges
in ripples sent ellipsing with the zebras'.
Bring your body round it, let the liquids
seep away the sand and lie supported.
You float and feel communion with the serâb,
your edges, hardened faces, smooth to curves
and all pulls, you sense, are infinitesimal;
each flea-sized spring a drain the size of sand.

The water seeps into its tiny sluices,
the gardens curl, compress themselves to dust.
You lie across a desert acre, await
sirocco, restitution, and sleep as sand.

TWO FOLLOWERS OF CADMUS
DEVOURED BY A DRAGON

Not a tooth, in truth,
a bone from the base of the brain
with the soul sealed in:

luz. And rattles round,
all recall and rage in the belly
bringing fire to the breath

and to our incarceration
in these carcass pieces.

     ~

What a way of death;
where there were no teeth
there were talons,

or soon to be talons,
or teeth, and still dreams
of teeth, and of compression

to this small still-sensate tomb,
this bone, this dragon-tooth.

     ~

We know its death
by the swamp air cooling
its unravelling guts,

and the ground into which
we are sown by the cold
and by the way that

no flesh but it burns
no eyes but it burns
and it burns and we loosen,

more bones unfold from this bone
and further from each, clack clack,
and a spine and on, ribs out like rhizomes,

hips and skull blossom each end
as clavicle spins into arms,
there is movement and loosening

soil, pushing with legs as they grow,
as tarsals and digits pop into being
like corn, and just as the jawbone

splits off from the face there is air,
there is surface, there is you –

~

you who sent us into the swamp
past birdsong into the silent clearings
and into the path of the dragon,

and now we are standing,
armed in your colours
to the ever so visible teeth,

amazed, just as you are amazed,
in mud, in dragon blood, in mist.

VATES

How long is it now we have spent in this time that consents to be no time
for signs or seers? Let us pass over fearful assent for the pentecostal
        jabber –

bring me hyssop and furze to this hill, take hands to stare the sky through
to where your icon is, join our pantheon, your icon to mine, a river, a
        raindrop,

scale so hard at this distance it makes no difference and gives no guarantees –
yours may be a butterfly with cyclones in its ambit, may be a thundercloud

keeping one person dry. See far as you can, let me be spyglass
or comfort as is your need, but know I am no more the way

than are you. What you need to know you never will, but let me hold you,
help you trust; there is faith in our hands held, we are all then each
        within every,

despite no sign but our own. No sign is not the sign for no, we believe
although no sign for yes will come, this being no sign, and find a way

leaving, as signs, our footprints as in dew.

EYES

Whose is this wetwalled cellar where the eyes
float live in jars? Where behind the discards
pile up, deflate, the aqueous humour spilt
and dried and fleshy shine of retina
on show, dulling? What if I were
to reach in a jar, gloved in the alcohol
soft give of eye? Thin skin of slime
against the glass, oogle bounce the eyes
against the fingers. I'd slip pickled eyeballs
into armpits, groin, to near the lymph nodes,
see myself fit. I'll be forgiven.

PICA

A garage and two magpies; friends,
these make the case we must be open
to what joy there is to find.

Symptoms of pica include cravings
for such non-food substances
as paint and flour and gravel.

Pica pica, these two may
be all that they are omen of,
all I can expect today.

CHILL

moon
as faint
as a misprint

one cold afternoon
in cloudless
november

air
freeze dried
so vibrissae shiver

and one believes
one's thoughts
immeasurable

IN GIRUM IMUS NOCTE ET CONSUMIMUR IGNI

We enter the circle at night and are consumed by fire.

Or we spin the small lit world around us like the sparrow
that flit through Bede's imagined meadhall, glimpsing fire.

And in the dark we fly on, unconsumed; how comforting to hope
that Edwin chose the right path, that we should aspire to sparrow
over resignation to the thought of nothing beyond the reach of fire.

Beyond the reach of firelight. The threat that dark fire can reach
beyond the meadhall light adds fear to the gift of manifest hope,
is the spot of shadow cast by the flight of the sparrow.
The bird flies beside the light; the moth hurls itself at fire.

Confusion of the cold moonfire and our cooking flame calls
the moth from moonlit flight, sets a moon the moth can reach
by veering round, and its smaller smaller circles of the fire
seem a straight line to its compass; it cannot know the hope
of escape, of recognising the exit of the non-stop sparrow

and what more faith in sense have we? Suppose we spiral in
unrecognised curves to a false focus, on come-hither calls
transposed to the visible; what feels like fledging to sparrow
may be scaling to moth. What quick apprehension hopes to reach
a point of certainty? We shape decisions on systems spun from hope
that each wingbeat of belief is on the path to window, not to fire.

That there is no fire. Not knowing whether further flight or night is in
the world beyond the window, our hope contains a further hope
and it all spirals out. The logic tells you there is nothing you would call
a starting point, but don't the stories let you feel that point is within
        reach?
Though no hands in the parable outstretch to stop the sparrow –

farewell, sparrow! – though none who tried would have had the reach
to manage, or has, they shaped the story to their hands, to fit in
their familiar grasp and bring belief into ergonomics they could call
cuð, translated to intelligible that promised hope

and made it no hope compared to the untranslatable that called
the metaphor into existence. Eternal truths demand a new way in
avoiding parables that dry to limescale, that make their reach

an absence of reach, a known motif distracting hearts in
like a stained-glass window that steals the aura of what calls

although it makes no call itself, and offers no way in.

EEL
April 2005

The spark that says it all starts, this time, was not
the news that Amen was the Pope's last word
and thus his life a prayer but the fish-flash response
but they would say that that zipped unbidden
as a wet dream through the tissues of my brain.
Watch me dodge the urge to eisegesis on that,
treat it as a monad fact. Also on the fact
the shame tastes somehow willed, or sentimental.

Another monad: I had just seen *a penitent's hand*
nailed to a cross in Santa Lucia, Philippines,
in an unofficial Easter ritual, and another,
that I cannot recall whether *where is the blood?*
or *where can that faith be found?* came first.
That this seemed a warm siren sounding out my Baltic.

Or a silent klaxon driving this week dogwhistle-mad,
a semi-secular week in which faith calls out
and, within, something I thought lost or jellied
flicks, shocks, in common time to whatever
sings in that Sargasso voice so like faith.
Go on, prise the brainpan up to peek
at elvers like electrons, all motion no presence
choreographed to this inaudible call.

Like faith, and like fear. I do not want a god through fear.
There's the word, then, are you brave enough
to leave it lowercased? So far, second voice.
Are you out of monads then? you're drifting
back to lyric. Thought I ought to warn you.
You're never out of monads. Here's another:

That I read about his silver crozier
stolen by a journalist with a typo,
leaving somewhere deafened a silver crow.
And that elsewhere I saw a comedian kick off
with *So, the pope walks into a bar* –
is it too early for that? That I felt no eel stir
for laughing at these. No Vatican victory roll
just yet, anyway. But what the eel has turned up:

That I have this image of my eyes coming clear
like angelic cheerleaders whisking off their pompoms;
and an image of what had seemed proof when faced
with this evangelical eyedrop mouldering to sophistry
in mouth-of-ashes weeks. I miss that dawning.
That I remember these like plot-points, not experience.

One I do remember – image of a logic class
and Cantor's theorem making clear that infinities
can be bigger than each other. Logician cheerleaders
this time. And all I recall is the clearing, not proof.
That this leaves me free of ashy mouthfuls,
but uncertain of my argument or premises
and thus reduced to absurd thoughts of souls
that must be infinite and infinitely divisible, hurrah.

Given the set of all sets of all cardinal numbers,
it's when we map an ordinal to each set; the set of sets
whose ordinal is not a member of the underlying set
cannot be represented by a member, who could not
then be a member, or vice-versa. Not sure that's right.
Cantors and cardinals come in bearing pompoms.

New monad. That I will write 'each moment of joy
is a prayer' although I know that pesky other voice
will jump in saying *do you think that saying
makes it so?* See? But I say 'so far', again,
which means I worship much and undirected
like a child's sun, joyous lines sine-curving
from my smiling face, smiles for blissful eyes,
without channel or conduit. *Bravo! Swami or swamp?*

Well, there's this feeling of standing in cinders
in standing water, the ashes in the mouth thing
that calls for someone to Cinderella me – the monad
isn't that I feel it but that I kind of want to.
That somewhere there should be a ball I am due at
with chandeliers and harps to lead the dance.

Which is probably some conga-line, some channel
to hop along in, strait and narrow through a wicket gate,
a path, a road, an icy course to luge along at speed
like those elvers hurtling through capillaries –
except it seems more like I stand and wait.
Like this pelican has, not the red patch whence
it feeds its young, but the red man saying stop
and the walker has no guarantee to shine green.

Lightbulbs break and burn out. Pff. Before that,
they only get their numinous shine because the gas
within the glass is too dopey to react. The lights
are on means no-one's home. Except the wire
is live and it's the dull surround that keeps it so.
The green man waits to be mainlined too.

And some extrapolation siren sounds. Monad me.
How about that I recall, quite recently, my lover
recalling how, quite recently, she found Jesus
had left traces on what she'd call history too.
That I love and stay unmarried yet. That love
has no theorem behind it but its cleared eyes
survive abandonments and arguments. That
ye love one another is the new commandment.

That despite that and the spark that said to start
it's not the Vicar nor quite who he's vicar for,
but love's arrow-flash that carols in this crisis
of lack of faith. *Oh, how much you like
that phrasing! But now you have this sense
of arms behind you do you fall?*

STONE GUITAR

~

Here in sorrow, mister sculpture, I turn to you
in some imaginary rendezvous. Both as handshake
and as heartbreak, here's my hand in greeting. Let's go.

~

It's not as if, I know, you knew him.
If your bloodless eternity could know
the hands of your sculptor, even.
If we can know if we have a sculptor.

If your eye can be more than a single
petrified blood cell, if it can perceive
these lives that skitter like thunderflies
ahead of your marmoreal chords.

Your more than real chords. If these
are all we are, if we are leitmotivs
in a long stone fugue on a stone guitar,
if we are more are less if we are.

~

The chair the flesh the grounding force
and the guitar the verb. A man is caught
between his gravity and artistry
the grasp of his feet and the urge to fly
and all become part of one another.

~

I play. I know the life and death of stones,
the *white to play and kill* of tsumegos.

What do you read ahead, mister statue,
the tune you carry slow as flattened stone

your flow your metamorphosis long forgotten
the chisel marks still raw in your long mind?

~

And you began in clay,
your lost maquette haunts
an absence in the lives
your absent eyes see.

An absent friend returns
to clay, remaining lives
unhaunted but recalling
life as he would make it.

~

To clay? to climb? Your mason known, you are
no afterthought of nature, no accident of genes.

All guitar. La chair est triste. The flesh that holds
only holds so long, holds long enough that we decide

how much we are guitar, how much we sink into chair.

~

All become part of one another. As flats
into marshland, as marshland to waterway,
as waterway to sea, as him to me. Each poem

that appears post mortem holds me still,
still, the cold shot through me in a stave
of frozen nocturne from the stone guitar.

~

The world a wet waterglass
and a Finger sets resonances
from the rim, rippling,
immeasurable and outside hearing;
the stone guitarist knows
the rhythms one must move to.

~

A blank eye, an absent face, an anamnesis
at the centre of your song. Or so in hope

but not in truth, you cannot be gravestone
to everyone however monumental your mason.

Not forget. Not remind. Your music glimmers,
lacquered in extrapolation; only elegies for me.

For anamnesis, apples. For you a music slower
than the long sine wave of a tree in growth.

~

The poem wants to call the apples
orphaned but the call of art alone
is a call of stone. There is still,
mister marble, a love for apples
and some will be gathered,
and some will fall to earth.

~

For apples are antonyms to stone; see
the kiss of flower to mouthful of flesh
to fall, and to your erythrocyte eye

it is fast as breathing, yes. For fallen flesh
leaves fragments that invert to shoots to roots
to future kisses, mouthfuls, further falls

and you are futureless if fixed. Not so, you'd say,
the sticky liquid flow not future but
a continuity, a legacy, an admission of death.

~

Fully aware, mister gravestone face,
this unreliable, unpolishable flesh
plays mayfly piccolo to your strings.

The particulate chords of your advice,
sifting immortality behind your frets,
mister intersecting planes,

cannot prevent these puny elegies
that change nothing.

~

The guitar and the man and the chair.
All become part of one another. The man's legs
are those of the chair. This is another step forward
in its total integration of one another.

I made a number of the pattern of the man, the chair.
The guitar and the man's legs are those of the chair.
All become part of the chair. This is the chair.
This is the man, the guitar is the man, the chair.

The guitar and the pattern of the chair. The guitar
is the torso of the man's legs are those of variations
on the chair. This is the man and the man
and the pattern of the pattern of which you are

perhaps the man and the most interesting
in its total integration.

~

Then there is nothing to understand.
Then there is only grasping after understanding,
then becoming one's own reason for another's reach.
Then we are passing breves on your particulate stave,
sounding, then softening, then silencing, then stopped.

~

All become, yes,
part of one another,
chair man guitar,
in the world
which will be renewed
guitar man chair
which will be
renewed in the world
man guitar chair
in which the world
will be renewed

~

The closing notes our little apple shapes
have waited for, no subtle afterthoughts
of nature, play at the still point, the false eye,
their particulate music, wishing nor death
nor pain. To forgive, to farewell, to future.

VALE

will make this for you make this beautiful
for you make this of watching the starlings
on neighbour roof corners and the several
songs of birds that hop unhawkmolested
through fields still stubbled nearby

will make of it beautiful of my first bullfinch
and of no fox no hawk today what is
for own sake beautiful beautiful for you
you leave a will to beauty in your wake

ALCYONE

Alcyone, headlong to clifftop, is becoming
a bird. Orange through aquamarine
behind her, liquefaction of speed,
her clothes stream as her feet are slashed
by sea grass. *'Ceyx!'* Son of light,
daughter of wind, lovers each side
the surface of sea, her grief leaps miles out
and fathoms down, just as the lees of his air
leapt to her bed, becoming in dreamstuff
his sodden shape; she knew by the brine
on his breath his death, threw unfastened on
the dress she had sewn to speed his return
and ran. And runs. Through palace gardens,
palisades, over paving, grass, gorse,

      and the edge. An ankh
      of herself she turns
      orange through aqua
      marine shrinks
      faster than distance
      would force her
      and that is a kingfisher
      that flies out to sea
      to a wet mate returning

and that is not the rosette of her clothes a nest
on the surface, nor is that blood on the rocks.
There are still days, days with the sea still enough
to nest on, that put storms aside, that become this day.

GLASS

    when
  the glass
that I use

    that
  holds water
admirably, that reflects

    light
  when sun
shines on it

    shatters
  I say
of course it

    is
  already broken
every damned minute

THE THIRD DREAM

Night's hand in my chest gone
and Dreamer Owen says I am set
    for the first dream. The right stone
will help you, will answer the palm
    of your hand. And between kale-furrows
it showed, a tear of sandstone, to daylight.

~

The salt-bathed stone bakes slowly,
in accordance with the strictures, to pure,
    cools by my cot, away from other souls.
We speak. We bring our souls in line.
    As Dreamer Owen says I ask *help me*
find your counterpart. And trust and hold and sleep.

~

Dreamer Owen says the drowning dream
is not uncommon, but mastery is rarely
    so rapid. I am rare. The second dream
is given, is to dream of nothing; not not-to-dream
    but dreaming with no object.
To meet another world without disguise.

~

Each morning now my sheets are salted
with the smallest shells, tiny starfish,
    krillbones. I do not know if this
is the third dream. I sleep with the stone
    on a shelf, wake with it to hand, and wake
each time I near the stove to heat it safe again.

MOUSE STATION

There is no sign here to say this was a station,
only the raised eye shape, a grey brick shuttle,
lashed with grass. Where the hole would be
a heap of mice roil and part to release a body,
naked, bleeding from a thousand tiny toeholes.
From its knees it raises its back straight and stands, a man,
irised by mouse eyes in moss destroying the lattice.

He shivers as a wind begins to scab
the punctuation of his back. The mice scrape in again,
narrowing the radius and unafraid his eyes keep closed
as they climb his body a skin more. Each foot
full-stops a button to the suit. Jump he thuds
uncertain between cold and rusted rails
and pace to pace he matches the sleepers.

Each step loosens the skin, pulls holes to teardrops,
till a total clench of mousepaws stops him
in their tracks. His hand out left is aware of the curve
of a station lintel wet with moss. He hauls
his self and skin to the platform, where the mice
reward him, sliding off. His body trembles more than he does.
Everywhere a hum comes entering the gut.

Not a hum now, a moan, the mice are pollen
on water or seem it. The first mouse-back crack
reveals a heavy foot, which snaps through rodents
to the man. Now only the *oh*, she is still
he puts out a hand to feel only wood and twine.
Its *aah* begins to move its tone around its register,
a woman, then, and his fingers find skin between bark.

His own flesh quivers to each mouse death.
The scratch of paw on wood and stamp, another.
His ribs ache. The tonic *ah* falls between
the notes, between his bones, and keeps him near still,
but steady enough to move his hand along the grain,
to find the throat between breast and helmet
and pause again

as the note changes. The word also and his eyelids
resist, resist, flit up to reveal two pupils each
over the torpedo nose and whiskers of more mice.
The wood creaks as she steps back swings in silence
and splays him across the rails. The sound is now
the scrabble of paws of mice as mice pour as if funnelled
on the body, holding in the greenstick arm, have him

climb back to his feet to face her clap her cork-bound hands
and begin that hum. Leaving the break they scatter
round his body, inscribing lines that dash the body through.
The first fall of inner lights steams tripes in the sun
and the mice collect a cairn of themselves
over the corpse as fallen. The hum stops as the pile subsides
and a red-spat flow limps fleeing through the rails.

MOONSWIM

shore
falls away
     sea
falls away
     save
the current you're in
uplifting still speeding
     moonwards
     moon face
     moon eye
          hare's eye
swings central
     spins blacker deeper
          nearer
     knowing what hares know
          – you

SALAMANDER

cheers l'chaim
sante slàinte
salamander!

all set:

breathing textiles finest filters
top-of-the-range victorinox
stout boots, stout stick
and the newest PDA
with imaging and GPS
and mayday beacon

– like you'll need it –

look, the path is easy
and leads right to the peak.

borborygmus shudders you
who knows most tremors are meaningless;
teporingo hoiks to haunches.

Dust kicks up from walking, one thing,
and dust drifts in the air – what's the mask for
if not for this? trying not to wipe it
like avoiding liplicking during a doughnut.

further you find behind the path an axolotl
crisped anhydrous
dehydrated dead
perfect crispy sculpture of itself

fascinating –
you take digicam snap
and PDA touchtype burst

you skip the shudder for
their stick figure eyedots, sockpuppet mouths

you miss teporingo
scavenging the crisp corpse
that could not read the tremor's signature

not dust so much as ashes, tiny cinderflecks
autofocus can't find which to focus on
tephromancy were it not discredited would say
ash says something's coming

poreclogged goretex,
poor self-sodden you

ash says where's the teporingo now?

teporingo burrow far downhill:
dead axolotl placed face out
and beyond, the noise and backflung scree
        of deeper burrowing

and the peak – no record but no shame either –
small sulphurous pool wrought thick with axolotls
uncanny unvulcanised flesh slithing over each other

ash says what do axolotls want?

extremophile fritillaries flit through thickening tephra swirls here;
harbingers or bringers, you would say
ash says you will never know
ash spirals in wake of ash-happy insects
           and you do not catch its holograph

palmpilot snarls with dust
can't steer you now
file not found
c:\>
c:\>_
c:\>
c:\>_
c:\>
c:\>_

and axolotls climb now from their pool
and ring the rim expectant, look up.

what noise have you made to make heads turn,
reflect you in eyes like fuel oil left to still to mirrors?
eyes that turn and take no interest?

this is what they're waiting for
this plume that spumes ash into air

and a pyroclasm climbs the rim and flows
faster than flowing, surging through slowed fronts
and elbowed through itself,
engulfs the waiting axolotls in ash,
in sulphur, in tangible heat
and each small form thrown airborne ignites, each muscle
           burns to ripcord,

soft strips back to sinew-sharp
and they do not extinguish but skip from cinder to cinder,
mephitic fireflies leaping clinker to bullet-fast pumice,

– teporingo hunkers down
deep behind its fireproof charm –

and you, whatever left of you who watched,
are become an ashen sculpture of yourself,
pumicepocked furnace-pinging claimed by flame
and carried with the salamanders past the lip.

SEA-GIRL WREATHED WITH SEAWEED

I have seen such things so deep my eyes are pearls,
such pretty things beyond the surf and reefs,
beyond the seals, the whales, the narwhals and down,
the rocks, the wrecks, the darkening, so deep
that the weeds dance in anglerfish light. Come see,

come reach from your raft to me, for I know the currents
that lie beneath these doldrums. I know where to lie
so that tides may take us further than one oar may.
Becalmed, to be still is to stay still, as lost as on land,
where you mistake danger and death for freedom.

Can you dive there? Can you rise? Is your weight taken,
your every gesture swathed in reaction to a caress? Join me,
make no choice but the water, be borne in the currents
and never choose wrong again. Join me, come to me, yes –
o, the brine of this first breath, I know, is acrid,

but these arms that hold you here are soft. The memories
that your lungs hold onto are substantial only as the foam
of breakers retreating always through the shingle. Nothing,
nothing, is so sweet as the second. It is a small price,
to be dead, to be free of the fear of becoming so.

RUIN

these wall-stones cause wonder   *wyrd* broke them
tore up the courtyards   titans' work decays
the roofs are rent   ruinous the towers
the high gate is smashed   cement burst with frost
the storm-havens shattered   sheared fallen
under-eaten by age   the earth's-grip has
the master-builders   buried perished
its hard grasp to hold   until a hundred generations
of people have gone   grey-mossed and red-stained
the walls long outlasted   one lordship after another
still stood under storms   stately but fell
the masonry remains yet   mauled by the weather

many on ————   ————————
grimly ground down   ————————
———————— shone   they ————
———————— ability   ancient craftworks
———————— a circle   in the skim ————
———————— brain could   have braided a sleek
brilliance in rings   a resourceful one twined
wallbraces from wires   in wonder together
the buildings were bright   the bath-houses plentiful
their roofs set sky-high   the hero-sounds loud
until that was altered   by all-mighty *wyrd*
the slain fell widely   and sickness-days came
all of the brave ones   borne off by death
their worship-halls became   waste places
as the city decayed   their care-takers sank
like their idols to earth   each edifice abandoned
and the red curves of tiles   tumbled away
from the rafters of the roof   the ruin subsided
to cairns of rubble   where countless ones once
shone in their war-gear   wine-glad and proud
looked on treasure, on silver   on trappings, on wealth

on gems cut with skill   and set into metalwork
on the bright city   of broad command
a stone building stood   to stream out hot water
wide in a wave   so a wall caught it all
in its bright bosom   where the baths were
hot to the heart   how convenient
so let flow ———   ————
the steaming water   over the stones' grey faces
to the ring-shaped pool   where the baths were
there is ————   ————
———————   that is a noble thing.
a house —————   a city ————
———————   ————

FROM THE CAVE PAINTING

Forgive the shoddy crafting – I have little time, here too the new have come,
their plates of clay, their tiny tools, their zeal to show us how. Too many
learn these marks that capture only sound, whose bison is two grunts,
two grunts, they will not feed on that. Remember where the language lies;

not in the words, but what they reach. Read this and recall;
will their sparrow-scratches bring rain, nurse crops from their husks,
bring fire from smoking hay? Will it last? It may be that language will sustain,
but I fear that we instead will pass, our hands the last to be language-stained.

If you read both language and their scritches do not read this; let the truth die
rather than be tamed to their spindling marks. If you believe, you can find us
in the cave in which the first mouth was first drawn, first drew breath.

NOTES

The emphases in the epigraph to 'Herb Robert' are the herbalists':
www.middlepath.com.au/plant/herb-robert_geranium-robertianum.php,
accessed September 2011.

The 'Serâb' is the inferior, or hot road, mirage.

'Glass' derives from Mark Epstein's *Psychotherapy Without the Self.*

'Sea-Girl Wreathed with Seaweed' – refers to 'The Love Song of
J. Alfred Prufrock', line 130, 'sea-girls wreathed with seaweed'.

'Ruin' translates from the Anglo-Saxon poem.

ANDREW BAILEY was born in London and raised in Northwich and Preston. He studied at the universities of Nottingham and Sheffield, lived in London for several years, and now lives in Sussex. He was one of the original editors for the Poetry Archive, and has also worked for the Poetry Society, Poetry International Web and a handful of fringe theatre companies. Poems have appeared widely, online and offline, in journals including *Poetry Review, Rialto, Ambit, Gists and Piths* and *Stand*. He was the 2005 winner of the Geoffrey Dearmer Prize.